© The Quilt Digest Press 1983. All rights reserved.
ISBN 0-913327-05-0 (1985 edition)
ISBN 0-913327-00-X (1983 edition)
ISSN 0740-4093
Library of Congress Catalog Card Number: 82-90743
Printed on 100 lb. Satin Kinfuji and 260g/m² Bon Ivory (cover)
by Nissha Printing Company, Ltd., Kyoto, Japan.
Color separations by Dai Nippon Printing Company, Ltd., Tokyo, Japan.
Book design and mechanicals completed by Kajun Graphics, San Francisco.
Typographical composition in Sabon by Gestype, San Francisco.
Editing assistance provided by Harold Nadel, San Francisco.
Photographs not specifically credited were provided by their owners.

Revised edition, 1985.
Second printing.

The Quilt Digest Press
955 Fourteenth Street
San Francisco 94114

THE QUILT DIGEST

THE QUILT DIGEST PRESS   SAN FRANCISCO   1

THIS is the revised edition of the inaugural volume of *The Quilt Digest*, first published in 1983. Putting it together for you was a pleasurable and rewarding experience. This annual book is our answer to a need we have long perceived: a journal where quilt lovers can offer their thoughts and discoveries. Toward this goal, *The Quilt Digest* is a journal for antique quilt devotees and contemporary quilt enthusiasts alike. Surely we can learn much from each other.

The quilt revival is leaving its infancy and entering adolescence. It is our hope that through these annual journals we can contribute to its coming of age. We will feel justified in our endeavor if *The Quilt Digest* stimulates appreciation and fosters understanding, heightening awareness among its readers.

On pages 70 and 71 you will find information about subsequent volumes of *The Quilt Digest* and other books about quilts which we publish. After you have read and viewed this inaugural volume, we hope that you will turn to these pages.

Contents

THE tendency of the last decade to evaluate nineteenth-century American quilts using primarily aesthetic criteria too often unties those subtle threads which bound the quiltmaker to her work. Her sensibilities extended beyond color and form; if we spread her quilted journal before us, it can offer us a reflection of a specific place and time.

The middle of that century found both country and quiltmaker at the height of their creative confidence. Western Expansion had become a national obsession and there had developed a new image of the American, one of courage and self-sufficiency. The log cabin came to be synonymous with self-reliance, ingenuity, practicality and optimism — traits that Frederick Jackson Turner would later consider among the dominant factors in the shaping of the American character.[1]

Not every woman who made a Log Cabin quilt was stitching into it personal experiences on the frontier, but wherever she lived and whatever her circumstances, she was surely caught up in the excitement of that patriotic preoccupation. The log cabin was the symbol of something that involved her emotional fibre if not her physical presence. But for the pioneer woman, the quilt would hold special significance. She was an intimate part of that great adventure and she chose to record it within the sphere she found most comfortable.

IN 1845, the editor of the New York *Morning News,* John L. O' Sullivan,

The Log Cabin

An American Quilt on the Western Frontier

··

by Sandi Fox

added a new phrase to the American vocabulary by announcing it to be "our manifest destiny to overspread and to possess the whole of the continent which Providence has given us for the . . . great experiment of liberty." It was the view that had been held by Thomas Jefferson, and it would determine the direction of an emerging nation.

A century earlier, settlers had begun to detach themselves from the eastern seaboard. Victory in the French and Indian Wars had opened the first narrow paths to internal migration, and by 1800 a wedge

based on the coastlands was pointing deep into the Mississippi Valley. Ribbons of civilization pushed steadily outward, pressing impatiently against a series of new frontiers. With the rapid acquisition of large areas of new land, the major boundaries fell: Texas in 1845; Oregon in 1846, following a long dispute with England over the western fur trade that was commemorated in the quilt pattern "Fifty-four Forty or Fight!"; California in 1848 by secession from Mexico; and additional portions of the Southwest through the Gadsden Purchase in 1853. What had begun slowly on foot had ended, on wheels, in a fevered race to the Pacific Ocean. Although the frontier would not close historically until 1890,[2] the great dream had been realized.

A man could not have entered those hostile environments had he not felt confident that beyond each new frontier he could provide shelter for his family with minimum tools, skill and money. From the beginning, a unique architectural adaptation allowed rapid expansion across the continent: it was a simple log cabin, and it was built wherever pioneers moved out to fulfill that Manifest Destiny. Even among the sod houses of the plains, or the native adobe of the Southwest, one found log cabins by the river or wherever timber was available.

Like the nation itself, the log cabin had its beginnings in the Old World. Swedish settlers had left a homeland similar in wooded intensity to this new country, and when they settled New Sweden in 1638 they brought with them the traditions of log dwellings.

As with all European concepts, either functional or emotional, the Swedish structures were modified to meet the needs and circumstances of the new environment. The roots of the American log cabin are deep in the Delaware Valley.

One man, with one simple tool, could utilize the material at hand to secure immediate protection against the elements and any physical dangers the forest might conceal. The axe was a vital tool to the frontiersman. With it he could clear the selected site, then shape and notch the fallen logs. The method of construction he would use would not require nails or spikes — an important consideration when nails were hand-wrought and expensive, and too heavy to consider adding to the contents of an already overloaded wagon or cart.

For the quiltmaker on the American frontier, the tools she required were likewise simple and few. She could carry in her apron pocket the needle, thread and scissors she would need to turn any available scraps of precious fabric into a Log Cabin of her liking.

Both builder and quiltmaker began with a simple and defined method of construction. In spite of the constraints of basic pattern and technique, each cabin and each quilt could emerge as a unique and personal expression of craftsmanship. With the cabin, the builder might select a variety of woods for special and studied reasons — oak or walnut for the logs that would rest on the foundation, walls of tall forest pine, or the cedar that was easily hewn and would fill

the cabin with a sweet aroma.[3] The size and shape of the log, the placement of window and door, the individual style of handmade shingles — each would give a particular cabin an individual character. With the quilt, its special singularity might be deter-

Log Cabin-Barn Raising, c. 1875, Missouri, 82 × 72 inches, containing over ten thousand logs, most of wool. Collection Levi Strauss & Co., San Francisco. Courtesy of Kiracofe and Kile, San Francisco.

mined by the width of the "log" strips that formed its pattern, or by the choice of fabrics. The early Log Cabin quilts reflected the availability of wool or homespun, or challis. But when economics and availability again allowed, the frontier woman would find her

8

greatest delight in printed cotton. Later, of course, the Victorian excesses of civilization would demand the tiniest strips of silks and velvets.

The methods by which both cabin and quilt were constructed bear remarkable similarities. The cabin foundation could be stones firmly mortared with clay, or piles of rocks, but great care would be taken with either method to rest the foundation on firm subsoil. Unlike her pieced quilt, in which the quiltmaker would simply sew pieces of fabric one to the other, the traditional Log Cabin quilt block was worked on its own solid foundation, in this case a piece of muslin or cotton remnant.

With both building and block, the point at which the hearth was constructed was decided by practical considerations, but the result was a subtle expression of those divisions of labor clearly set forth within the pioneer family. The man was to provide shelter and protection for those in his care, and in his cabin the hearth and chimney were constructed only after the log walls were in place. The woman was the dominant figure in household affairs and, when she worked her Log Cabin, the "fireplace" forming the center of each unit was always the first piece to be sewn to the foundation block.

The fireplace was critical to the early settler and, without the convenience of matches, was usually kept burning day and night. It was used for cooking, light and warmth. The constancy and importance of the fireplace was affirmed by the quilt-maker, for even when the "log" strips in the block were of diverse and jumbled colors, that central symbolic square of cloth was always (as far as her resources would allow) constant in color throughout the quilt. Red was the obvious and preferred color, although yellow was sometimes used to suggest the function of the cabin as a light or beacon in the wilderness.

That center square was firmly sewn to the foundation block, and succeeding logs were sewn around it in an interlocking manner. The log was cut and shaped by an often crude pair of scissors, then placed face down and sewn through any preceding logs into

Log Cabin-Straight Furrow cradle quilt,
© 1980 Sandi Fox, 23¼ × 27¾ inches, cottons.
Collection of Mr. and Mrs. Franklin Knowlton.

the foundation. Once in place, each log was pressed back, ready to accept another layer of logs. As with the cabin, when properly put in place each log would strengthen and reinforce the other.

As she joined the individual blocks, one to the other, to arrange them in the classic variations of the Log Cabin quilt, she was in fact setting down her visual impressions of that critical segment of American history. We can observe in the pattern variations of those quilts an abstraction of the physical realities of her surroundings and note certain elements of social development on the western frontier.

The basic block in the quilt's construction was a square, visually divided diagonally into light and dark strips. Those standard blocks could then be arranged in a diverse number of strong graphic designs. In the most standard Log Cabin pattern, four blocks are joined together in repetitive groups of four. These in turn form alternating light and dark squares, on point, interlocked but each visually independent. In each block there is a strong sense of containment and, indeed, the early cabin represented just that. If Western Expansion was to succeed, each family unit must be self-sufficient. Survival itself would depend on individual performance for the good of all. At no time has the American family unit been so strong, so necessary. Single blocks of light and activity formed distinct boundaries against the wilderness:

· The dwelling in which the emigrants live has no internal division and no storehouse. The whole

9

family comes to seek shelter of an evening in the single room which it contains. This dwelling forms as it were a little world of its own. It is an ark of civilisation lost in the middle of an ocean of leaves, it is a sort of oasis in the desert. A hundred paces beyond it is the everlasting forest stretching its shade around it and solitude begins again.[4]

The individual structures provided stepping stones across a continent, but alone they would never cement a nation. Those solitary cabins in the wilderness must provide the nucleus for the small settlements that would be necessary to the success of the Great Experiment. Cabin raisings were not merely social courtesies. They were a man's duty to both his neighbors and his nation. The Barn Raising pattern (expanding diamonds of light and dark) celebrates the social gatherings in which pioneer women often found emotional sustenance, but it also records a necessary step in frontier survival. The first log forts did not house militia; they were log cabins clustered together by men who must defend themselves and, in so doing, protect the nation.

The Straight Furrow pattern, strong slashes of light and dark across the diagonal line of the quilt, acknowledged the pioneer's dependence on each overturned row of earth. This was an agricultural society, and the unit in that tight little cabin must produce whatever it would need to sustain itself. Of necessity, a woman often worked beside her husband during the first, difficult plantings, but as soon as it was possible to do so she moved back into her own sphere, returning eagerly to "woman's work" as much

by choice as by the dictates of tradition. She would, however, remain the keeper of a garden, and her connection to the soil continued apace with the cycle of the seasons around which pioneer life revolved.

When fields and pasture had been cleared, the resulting logs were put to essential use. Fences were needed to protect animals and fowl and the beginnings of a good crop from the predators of the encroaching forest. "Worm" fences (split rails stacked to a height of about five feet) enclosed cabin, outbuildings and fields, and are quite literally represented in the Log Cabin Zig Zag pattern.

The Courthouse Steps pattern, with its unique placement of light and dark logs, acknowledges the formalities of government observed even in those early, loosely formed communities. Charlotte, North Carolina, Decatur, Illinois, Steubenville, Ohio — these and others established early courts sitting in log buildings,[5] dispensing the fledgling forms of government to an expanding nation.

The bright calicoes of her quilt might mask harsher realities. For the pioneer wife, the move away from family and friends was almost always an emotionally devastating experience, and the choice to emigrate was not always a decision in which she had been allowed to participate. The dark woods held the constant possibility of physical danger. The forces of nature were always threatening to overwhelm even the greatest personal effort. In one of the most inventive and ambitious of the Log Cabin pattern var-

iations, she reached back to remembered refinements. The pineapple had long been considered the symbol of hospitality. On the eastern seaboard it had been worked by the hands of men — carved as finials, etched on glass, formed in silver. In the new environment of the frontier, the symbol for hospitality was a simple latchstring hung outside the cabin door. In developing the Pineapple pattern on her quilt, she was perhaps reaching back to softer times. The materials she chose were, of course, more appropriate to her new life, and the pattern that emerged showed the vigorous simplification that would come to characterize American design.

When she arranged her fabric in this pattern, but extended one immense block to the very edge of her quilt, the pattern became Windmill Blades and her work was once again tied to the image of the frontier.

As pioneer families moved away from the east coast, they would adapt, alter and in many cases simply abandon strong European cultural influences. They had brought with them across the Atlantic ethnic memories and traditions that in the course of Western Expansion would be woven into the very fabric of this new country. Each frontier was a renewal of effort and often demanded that even traditions already Americanized be reshaped. The Log Cabin quilt is a manifestation of those changes.

On the eastern seaboard of the early nineteenth century, one could generally ascertain the quiltmaker's place in society by her selection of fabric and technique. A woman

Log Cabin-Light and Dark with Zig Zag treatment, c. 1910, Holmes County (Ohio) Amish, 68 × 77 inches, wools and black cotton sateen. BankAmerica Corporation Art Collection, San Francisco. Courtesy of Kiracofe and Kile, San Francisco.

of the upper class both by location and economic status would have access to imported cloth, to the printed fabrics so much to her liking. The result might be a finely cut and stitched Broderie Perse. If her husband was a man of means, she need not rely on scraps and remnants, but could instead purchase new, whole pieces of cloth. If she had others to attend to her housewifely assignments, her time could be spent in adding an infinite number of tiny stitches to the background fill of her quilted work.

Similar considerations would of course be true on the western frontier, but the distinctions between rich and poor were blurred, both by the new concepts of social democracy and by the fact that even where there was wealth there was little to buy. An all-white quilt, delicately stitched and stuffed, would hardly be a realistic undertaking for a woman in a 15 × 18 foot cabin with a dirt floor. In addition, society on the early frontier was distinguished by a lack of pretension:

> Even those with a few choice possessions apologized; carpets were excused as "one way to hide the dirt," a mahogany table as "dreadful plaguy to scour."[6]

With such social standards, a woman would hardly risk offending the few women visitors she might hope to have by working on a quilt of great extravagance.

The Log Cabin quilt would be ideally suited to the idea of the frontier as the great leveler. The same fabric would no doubt be available to all. Just as class distinctions would inevitably develop within this experi-

Log Cabin-Pineapple crib quilt, © 1980 Sandi Fox, 40 × 40 inches, cottons. Collection of Ed and Marsha Bronsky.

ment in equality, the vanity of a fine needle-woman would no doubt triumph but, as with the social and economic distinctions that might emerge, here her status would be measured by her skill. On even the most humble Log Cabin quilt, the cut of the cloth could be true, the stitch could be even and small.

And this was the quilt for this time and place. Other than her own homespun, fabric was generally unavailable, and the Log Cabin could utilize each tiny narrow scrap of precious cotton "store-bought." She was working in small individual units of design that could easily be held in her lap when the whole family was gathered in that small cabin. If her own cotton patch was not yet producing, because the strips were sewn to a foundation block a batting was not absolutely necessary. If the demands of her daily activities weighed too heavily, the absence of a bat meant it need not be quilted.

And if the thought of a handsome applique quilt for "best" came to mind, it could be tucked away, for the primitive cabin in which she found herself was never meant to be more than temporary. A European traveler would assume that to be true:

> And in fact the log cabin is only a temporary shelter for the American, a concession circumstances have forced on him for the moment. When the fields that surround him are in full production, and the new owner has time to concern himself with the amenities of life, a more spacious dwelling and one better adapted to his needs will replace the log-house and make a home for those numerous children who will also go out one day to make themselves a dwelling in the wilderness.[7]

And if she were to bear it all, she would have to believe it to be true:

Dear Brother and Sister:
It is a long time since we have seen each other but I have not forgotten you altho many miles of land and water separate us. . . .we live in a dry cabbin it has two rooms and is verry comfortable is as good as the rest of our neighbors have so I am content with it till we can have a better one. . . .
Yours,
Mary M. Colby[8]

But illness, or death, or the elements often intervened in even the most modest expectations, and a cabin (in tribute to the craftsman who made it) might be required to shelter generations of her children and grandchildren. A Log Cabin quilt (in quiet tribute to *her* craftsmanship) might be all that remained to remind them of her. The Industrial Revolution had quickened the decline in the work of the hands. For the quiltmaker, her creative moment was about to pass.

THOSE early settlers on the frontier, their number swollen with new emigrants and with their own families, soon became a decisive factor in national politics. Andrew Jackson, the first president to have been born in a log cabin, was swept into office by this new constituency. William Henry Harrison recognized the effectiveness of the log cabin as a political symbol and made it the theme of his 1840 campaign, even though he had in fact been born in a mansion in Tidewater Virginia.

It was one of many myths surrounding the western frontier. Perhaps America was never as good or as innocent as Turner thought it to be. The families we imagine forging strong family bonds around a blazing fireplace deep in some piney woods may have shared merely practical rather than emotional ties. Not all women were saints in sunbonnets[9] and not all men matched those mountains. But in the middle of the nineteenth century, that is what they perceived themselves and this country to be. The Log Cabin quilt is a fragment of America's great adventure, a suggestion of what we wanted to be rather than of what we became.

A detailed portion of a Log Cabin-Windmill Blades, c. 1880, Lancaster County, Pennsylvania, primarily wools. Collection of Jack Woody and Tom Long, Altadena, California. Courtesy of Kiracofe and Kile, San Francisco.

REFERENCE LIST

1. Frederick Jackson Turner, *The Frontier in American History* (New York: Henry Holt and Company, 1920).

2. John A. Hawgood, *America's Western Frontiers* (New York: Alfred A. Knopf, 1967), chapter XII.

3. Alex W. Bealer and John O. Ellis, *The Log Cabin: Homes of the American Wilderness* (Barre, Massachusetts: Barre Publishing, 1979), pp. 36-37.

4. Alexis de Tocqueville, *Journey to America* (New Haven: Yale University Press, 1960), p. 341.

5. Clinton A. Weslager, *The Log Cabin in America* (New Brunswick: Rutgers University Press, 1969), p. 69.

6. Ray A. Billington, *The Frontier in American Thought and Character* (New York: Holt, Rinehart and Winston, Inc., 1972), chapter XII.

7. De Tocqueville, p. 334.

8. Lillian Schlissel, *Women's Diaries of the Westward Journey* (New York: Schocken Books, 1982), p. 157.

9. Dee Brown, *The Gentle Tamers* (Lincoln: University of Nebraska Press, 1958), chapter I.

SANDI FOX is a quilt scholar and quiltmaker. Her work in both fields has been supported by grants from the National Endowment for the Arts and the California Arts Council. She has served as curator for five major exhibitions of nineteenth-century American quilts in the United States and abroad, and is the author of two important exhibition catalogues. One of ten distinguished contemporary craftsmen selected by ABC to be featured in its documentary series *Handmade in America*, her own work is included in numerous private and corporate collections.

Lydia (age 94) Bontrager's sewing corner

14

AMISH INTERIORS
PHOTOGRAPHS BY SUSAN EINSTEIN

POSING for photographs is specifically forbidden by Amish law. Even so, the passive, non-resistant Amish people do not object actively to being photographed. If asked, the Amish man or woman politely refuses, tempting the photographer to sneak shots with a long lens in hopes that the intended subject is unaware.

Susan Einstein resides in an Old Order Amish community, affording her a rare opportunity to learn about these private people, but requiring her to respect their beliefs. Her sensitivity to their way of life, combined with a belief that much can be learned about a family by the environment it creates, has led her to document the interiors of Amish homes.

These photographs are emphatically clear and detailed. While each object in a scene contributes to an understanding of the Amish, some aspects seem incongruous. Craftsmanship has given way to practicality and, as farms are passed along to a son or daughter, each generation takes its turn at remodeling to meet new needs and reduce maintenance. Her home is an Amish woman's domain, and her homemaker's pride is evidenced by these immaculate interiors. In sharp contrast is the washroom of the seventy-three-year-old bachelor whose daily energies are spent outside, caring for his enormous garden. Somewhere in between is the teenager's room. Signs decorating his walls are ironic in the midst of Amish order, yet they foretell the few years of liberation he will be allowed before joining the church.

Driving through the Amish countryside, travelers are excited by complex farms — entire communities within themselves. For passersby, however, the exterior is all that is seen. These photographs are a rare opportunity to go behind that exterior and add to our understanding of contemporary Amish life.

—DAVID POTTINGER

SUSAN EINSTEIN is a free-lance commercial photographer based in Honeyville, Indiana.

DAVID POTTINGER is an American folk art dealer and collector. He is the author of *Quilts from the Indiana Amish: A Regional Collection*, published by E. P. Dutton.

Child's china cabinet on Edna Borkholder's porch

Manas and Mary Hochstetler's "daddy" house

17

Elmer T. Miller's bedroom

Bachelor Eli Hochstetler, Jr.'s washroom

Stanley Miller and Edna Knepp's wedding table

Church at Alvin Miller's house

LaVern (age 14) Borkholder's bedroom

Will and Ada Lambright's living room

Surviving without Selling Out

Thoughts from a Quilt Artist's Journal by Michael James

W^E live in an age in which it is difficult for an artist to create and survive without some compromise: the temptations are everywhere, waiting. It is easier to please than to challenge and stimulate. The artist who remains true to himself (or herself) and to his work examines constantly. Is the work an honest image? Does it attract through powerful emotional and visual dynamism, or through gimmicks and trendy devices? In short, does the work have integrity? An artist keeps questioning, because his work should represent his best effort at the particular moment. It should even leap ahead to explore alternatives and new possibilities. Otherwise, the artist traps himself by following the familiar, comfortable, "sure-to-please" path.

If he stays aware of the potential pitfalls and is willing to avoid them, an artist can challenge the "real world" of commerce. And, though the difficulties I encounter in designing and producing a quilt pale next to writing about my work, I know that quiltmakers need to share with each other their experiences with the outside world.

For example, my feelings about galleries are, at best, ambivalent. Generally, I feel very uncomfortable about showing my work in a commercial gallery; I sometimes fear my work has been compromised when I see an exhibit in which it is included. The focus on sales in most galleries overshadows the work itself. With the

exception of an occasional commission, I don't make a quilt to sell or to meet a gallery contract quota; I make it to express ideas, to work out design concerns, to sustain and develop a larger body of work.

I make quilts because I enjoy the processes and the materials. The images I create reflect my personality and attitudes, and so my work is also a self-portrait and a sort of diary. My works are unique, each different in size, in technique, in image. Each takes from three weeks to more than six months to complete, and can easily represent six hundred hours of work. Even at the modest professional wage of ten dollars an hour, the return on six months of quiltmaking is not exorbitant.

In view of the nature of the work and the time spent on it, I find selling directly from my studio to be practical and profitable, while selling through galleries has been neither. In fact, not one of my quilts has yet been sold off the wall of a commercial gallery. I think the reason for that is simple: the high mark-up of a gallery places the price beyond the realistic market value of the work. When a gallery doubles the price of a consigned piece, the actual mark-up is one hundred per cent. Each of the galleries I have dealt with uses this formula, but unwaveringly describes the mark-up as fifty per cent, mathematics notwithstanding. In fact, a true fifty per cent mark-up would reflect a more equitable arrangement between artist and agent, in light of their respective roles. It would also increase the salability of the work. Few galleries faced with high overhead and low sales volume would agree, however.

One art consultant has successfully placed four of my quilts in corporate collections only after numerous presentations and in-

---

Scene from an Egyptian Rendezvous with Kites Flying, © 1982 Michael James, *60 × 60 inches, pieced and appliqued by machine in cottons, quilted by hand and machine. Private collection.*

25

Interweave I, © 1982 *Michael James, 38 × 38 inches, pieced and quilted by machine in cottons. Private collection.*

tensive selling; in this case, the agent clearly earned the commission. These successful sales were due in large part to the agent's enjoyment and belief in the worth of those quilts. Such an agent is indispensable to any artist who believes strongly in the validity and merit of his work. Nevertheless, I've yet to encounter an agent who doesn't apply some pressure, however subtle, for works of a particular size, or of specific colors, or in a visual mode that has already drawn enthusiastic response. Witness a letter I received in May of 1982:

> Thank you so much for sending the quilts. . . .We have shown them a couple of weeks. . .but the response hasn't been too good since the colors are so pink and green. I think most people thought of your work as being stronger and tougher in color. Nevertheless, they are very pretty and well thought out. We have returned them UPS, and they should be there soon.

Thus, agents ask me to make it easy for them to sell my work. If they could make it easy for me to create the work without sacrificing its integrity and personality, we might strike a bargain.

Commissions are, I believe, a more congenial brand of commerce. My first commissioned work was proposed by an architect designing a suburban Boston bank. I faced a new challenge and the chance to evaluate my feelings about it; at the same time, I had a reason to work on a relatively large scale and, for the first time, in a long rectangular format. Still, I faced the project with trepidation. Would the client want to impose limitations of size, color, or technique? Fortunately not. I was only asked to consider the intended hanging space and the surrounding furnishings. This artistic independence is the ideal foundation upon which to build a commission agreement. It improves the chances that the client will get a quilt in which both maker and buyer can take pride.

For several weeks I toyed with various thematic ideas, and finally I decided to develop a curvilinear composition based on the four seasons. I'd wanted to explore that subject for some time, and the rectangular format would allow a sequential development of the image. I considered the audience—the bank's employees and customers—and the locale. In New England, seasonal changes are striking and important.

The Seasons, © 1981 Michael James, 4½ × 15 feet, machine-pieced and hand-quilted cottons, satin acetate and cotton velveteen. Collection of Waltham (Massachusetts) Federal Savings and Loan Association.

I submitted a maquette of the piece but couldn't wait for final approval before I actually began working on the quilt: I had already begun thinking of "The Seasons" as my next work, and couldn't put off work for a month to await the approval. Proceeding without a contract with the client was unprofessional, but I felt right about the work and feared that a delay might diminish my enthusiasm. Within two weeks, the top of the quilt was completed. I made up my mind to complete the quilt even if its design was rejected. Final approval arrived two weeks later. The design of the quilting, and the hand-quilting itself, took seven more months.

To preserve my peace of mind, I now ask for a written agreement for a prospective commission. Such an agreement covers the process of designing the work as well as its execution. The client is expected to pay a fee for any sketches or maquettes. Installment payments for the quilt include an advance fee, a mid-completion payment, and the final payment upon delivery.

Apart from commissions and sales of individual works, teaching can allow a quilt artist to fill in the economic empty spaces. Although I find it a sacrifice to be away from my family and sometimes find traveling exhausting, the real struggle for a teacher is to have something of substance to offer a student. Most students seem to demand tangibles, such as a color formula or a system for organizing a geometric composition. Such devices can be put to immediate use: they give the student the feeling that he's getting his money's worth. They deceive, however, because they don't provide substance or insight; they provide only facility.

Certainly there is value in understanding how green affects red; there is greater value in understanding how red and green can express an attitude or thought or emotion, and how they can elicit

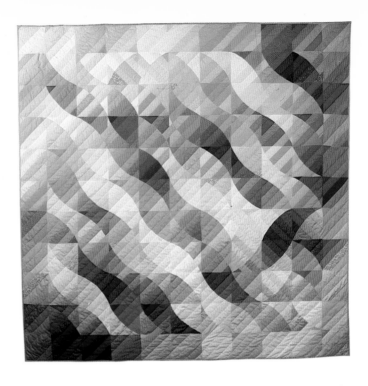

Interweave II, © 1982 Michael James, 68 × 68 inches, pieced and quilted by
machine in cottons.

Interweave III, © 1982 Michael James, 70½ × 71½ inches,
pieced and quilted by machine in cottons.

intellectual and emotional responses in the viewer. An artist not only orchestrates theories and design elements, tools and techniques; he also plays upon the audience's emotions and manipulates their responses. Therein lies his power. To teach someone how to begin to employ that power is ultimately of greater value than to teach a color rule or a device of spatial illusion.

An artist changes and grows constantly. So does his work. Yet, underlying all, an artist must believe in himself, must believe that his work is worth doing for its own sake. Each day an artist faces uncertainty, disappointment, self-doubt and failure. But an essential belief in himself and his work will bring him back to his studio to continue, or to start over. This self-appreciation must always be active inside an artist as he faces the world and its commerce. If an artist believes in the intrinsic value of his work, commerce will find its place in his world, and not vice versa.

MICHAEL JAMES is a quilt artist and the author of two important guides to contemporary quiltmaking, *The Quiltmaker's Handbook* and *The Second Quiltmaker's Handbook*, both published by Prentice-Hall. He is the recipient of Craftsmen's Fellowships from the National Endowment for the Arts and the Boston Artists' Foundation. His work has been exhibited internationally, and is included in numerous private and corporate collections. In autumn 1983, the Worcester (Massachusetts) Craft Center presented a retrospective exhibition of his first ten years of quiltmaking.

Interweave IV, © *1982 Michael James, 38 × 38 inches, pieced and quilted by machine in cottons. Private collection.*

SHOWCASE

COMPILED BY RODERICK KIRACOFE

Hearts, by Jacqueline Eichhorn, Centerville, Indiana, completed February 14, 1982, 42 × 44 inches, appliqued cottons. The symbols found on this quilt are highly personal: Jacqueline Eichhorn is an avid gardener; and her cat, Elsa, has the place of honor atop the Eichhorn home. Collection of the quiltmaker.

Tumbling Blocks variation, by Margaret Younglove Calvert, Bowling Green, Kentucky, c. 1870, 72 × 77 inches, pieced cottons, silks, wools and mohairs. Collection of The Kentucky Museum, Bowling Green, Kentucky. This quilt is one of forty-four works highlighted in *Kentucky Quilts 1800-1900*, published by The Kentucky Quilt Project, Inc., 127 West Ormsby, Louisville 40203.

President's Quilt, 1852, eastern United States, 76 × 76 inches, pieced and appliqued cottons. Techniques include padding, embroidery and ink work. The Mariner's Compasses surrounding the central eagle motif contain, in cross-stitch, the first initials and surnames of the first thirteen presidents of the United States. Private collection.

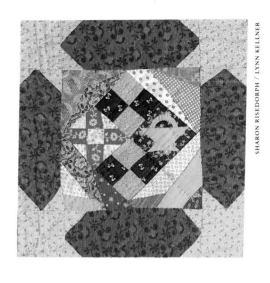

Sampler, c. 1880-1890, Pennsylvania, 72 × 78 inches, pieced cotton prints. Collection of Great Expectations, Houston. Courtesy of M. Finkel & Daughter, Philadelphia.

*B*ars, by Sarah Beiler, Paradise (Pennsylvania) Amish, c. 1925-1930, 78 × 78 inches, pieced wools. Made for Rachel Beiler Lantz, Sarah's daughter. The baskets quilted in the outer border and corner blocks are filled with fruit. "Sarah Beiler" is signed in script quilting in the outer border. Collection of Dr. and Mrs. Donald M. Herr.

Forty-Eleven, © 1982
Sonya Lee Barrington,
San Francisco, 56 × 56
inches, machine-pieced
cottons and poly-cottons.
Hand-quilted by Barbara
Wolfington, Garden
Valley, California.
Collection of Sonya Lee
Barrington.

Album, c. 1840-1850, Baltimore, Maryland, 74 × 75 inches, appliqued and pieced cottons. Techniques include padding, embroidery and reverse applique. Indistinguishable names and dates, and "Baltimore," appear on three blocks in ink. A fourth block is signed "Annabele A. Wade." Collection of Dr. and Mrs. Donald M. Herr.

Laurel Leaves crib quilt, by Kazi Pitelka, Los Angeles, 1982, 31 × 31 inches, appliqued, padded and stuffed cottons. Collection of the quiltmaker.

*L*os Angeles and Vicinity, by Judy Mathieson, Woodland Hills, California, 1982, 72 × 96 inches, pieced from over three hundred printed fabrics. This work is an elaboration of a Southern California AAA map. Its maker has personalized her rendition by indicating places of interest. In the detail, for example, one can find Dodger Stadium, Hollywood, the Griffith Park Planetarium, Marina del Rey and, indicated by tiny airplanes, Los Angeles International Airport. Collection of the quiltmaker.

Central Medallion, by
Jacqueline Eichhorn,
Centerville, Indiana,
completed September 10,
1981, 84 × 84 inches,
pieced cottons. Collection
of the quiltmaker.

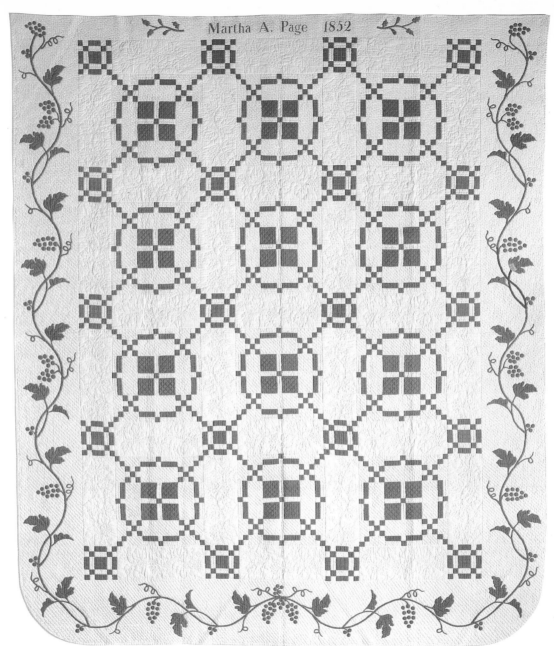

Burgoyne Surrounded, 1852, New England, 82 × 85 inches, pieced and appliqued cottons. "Martha A. Page 1852" is rendered in reverse applique. Private collection. Courtesy of Pilgrim/ Roy, San Francisco.

40

*S*tar *of Bethlehem,*
c. 1840, Pennsylvania or
Maryland, 91 × 93
inches, pieced and appli-
qued cottons. A floral
basket is quilted in the
center of each rose
wreath. Collection of
Dr. and Mrs. Donald M.
Herr.

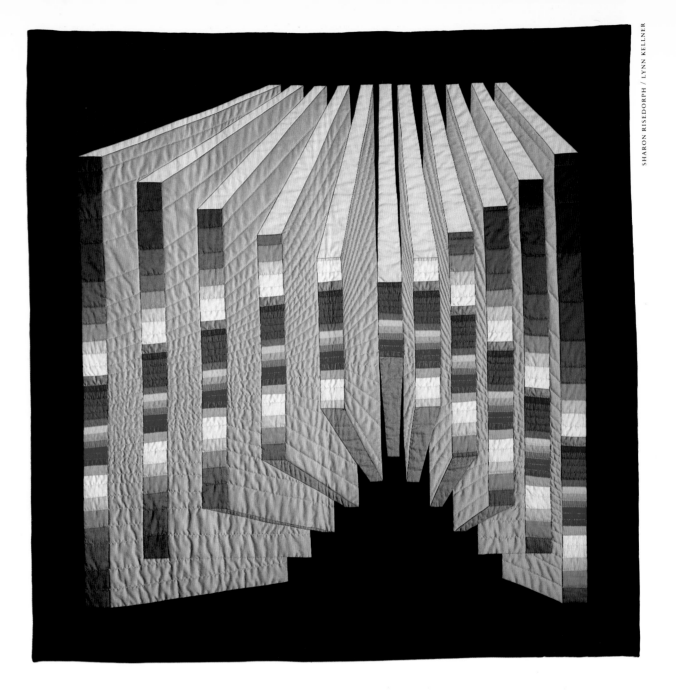

Night Rainbow V: "The Secondary Bow," © 1982 Chris Wolf Edmonds, Lawrence, Kansas, 50 × 50 inches, pieced cottons, quilted by hand and machine. Collection of the quiltmaker.

Crazy, by Emma Bull, 1893, Salt Lake City, Utah, 73 × 84 inches, predominantly silks and velvets. Among the many images are the Mormon Temple and Utah's bee-hive symbol. Initialed by the quiltmaker. Collection of Utah State Historical Society — Museum Services, Salt Lake City.

43

Wild Flowers, © 1981
Elizabeth Voris, Rancho
Palos Verdes, California,
98 × 98 inches, pieced
and appliqued cottons.
Multilayered applique
technique. Signed and
dated in embroidery.
Collection of the
quiltmaker.

*D*electable Mountains, c. 1850, the Herr family, Berks County, Pennsylvania, 87 × 91 inches, pieced cotton prints. BankAmerica Art Collection, San Francisco. Courtesy of Kiracofe and Kile, San Francisco.

SHARON RISEDORPH / LYNN KELLNER

Triad #6, by Leslie Carabas, Berkeley, California, 1981, 58 × 72 inches, machine-pieced cottons. Hand-quilted by Mattie Raber, Charm, Ohio. Signed by both quiltmakers. Collection of Leslie Carabas.

String Star, c. 1900-1920, La Grange County (Indiana) Amish, 86 × 71 inches, pieced wools. "M J Bontrager" is signed in script embroidery near the center of the quilt. Collection of Don and Faye Walters, Goshen, Indiana.

47

Leaves summer spread, c. 1850, New England, 95 × 95 inches, appliqued cotton with padded stems. Private collection. Courtesy of Kiracofe and Kile, San Francisco. (See cover for a detail of this quilt.)

Dawn, by Jan Myers, Minneapolis, 1981, 39 × 42 inches, pieced and quilted by machine in cotton muslins, hand-dyed with procion dyes. Collection of Margaret and Ray Davis, Atlanta, Georgia. Courtesy of Image South Gallery, Atlanta, Georgia.

49

The Reiter Quilt: A Family Story in Cloth

by Julie Silber

I have long believed that quilts, the work of hands, are among our richest tools in uncovering the lives and experiences of everyday women in an earlier America. Women are the "spectacular casualties" of traditional history.[1] For the most part, history books tell us of wealth, power and documents. Museums are filled with "important" objects — the Dupont highboy, General Sherman's uniform, Warren Harding's birth certificate. We are only now searching to understand what daily life was really like for our mothers and grandmothers. Quilts reflect our past, since they were made by virtually all nineteenth-century women, regardless of age, region or class. They were highly valued by the women who made them and the people who lived with them. Unlike most of women's domestic work, which leaves no permanent material traces, quilts endure. And although what we have left is not entirely representative of what was made, there are still many wonderful examples of old quilts for us to look at. They are beautiful objects, but much more. Beneath their surfaces are layers upon layers of feeling and meaning. Lovingly and thoughtfully examined, they reveal clues to the intricate world of the female past and our present.

I am always a bit nervous but excited when someone decides she wants to show me her family quilt. And so it was in 1976 when Leba Wine came into my shop. I had participated in this sharing ritual many times before, but I was not prepared for what I saw that day. Leba unfolded a beautiful album quilt or, more precisely, what I imagined had been one. Leba's quilt was in three pieces. My feelings were intense. I was impressed with the design's individuality and power, and moved by the maker's spirit. I was also very curious. Questions rushed into my mind. Who made this distinctive quilt? What kind of woman was she? Was this striking quilt made for a special occasion or to commemorate a milestone? What were the underlying meanings of the quilt's unusual images? Could the maker have been Jewish, like her descendant who stood before me? And why had this masterful work been cut into three pieces, yet carefully preserved in that peculiar state?

The Reiter quilt is a large piece, and quite impressive. It is an appliqued album quilt on a white cotton background with sixteen individual pattern blocks, the whole surrounded by a lush vine-and-flower border. The fabrics, which suggest the late nineteenth century, are solid red, yellow, orange and green, with only a few printed pieces. Black, a color rarely used in applique quilts, appears in five places: three animal and two human figures. Most of the sixteen pattern blocks are variations of floral motifs; only four have forms other than vegetation as their dominant theme. There are no purely geometric designs. Many of the appliqued pieces are embellished with embroidery which outlines or details the images. Many of the colored pieces are heavily padded, creating a plump, dimensional effect. Unlike some album quilts, which are formal and

Album, by Katie Friedman Reiter and Liebe Friedman, McKeesport, Pennsylvania, c. 1891-1892, 101 × 101 inches, appliqued cottons and wools. Collection of Theresa Reiter Gross.

elegant, this one has nothing of the prim or pretentious about it. There is not a trace of reticence. It is vibrant with life. Made by Leba's grandmother, Katie Friedman Reiter, with the aid of Leba's great-grandmother, Liebe Gross Friedman, its story, as pieced together by the family, begins in Europe.

Katie Friedman was born in 1873 in Czaklo, Slovakia, part of the Austro-Hungarian Empire. In the year Katie was born, the Vienna stock market crashed, marking the start of a twenty-year depression in east-central Europe. Life was especially difficult for Jews during that era of intense national rivalries. Anti-Semitism ran rampant. Leba tells of her paternal great-grandfather's death in the 1860s: "The sport in Hungary was killing rich Jews. He was sitting at the dining room table with his wife and seven sons, and somebody came along and shot him through the window. And that's how he died."

Katie's mother, Liebe, was widowed in 1882, and when she remarried the next year, Katie's life went from bad to worse. The new stepfather was "a swindler," and Katie's two stepbrothers were cruel. They would tie her to one side of a water-turn wheel, with a mule on the other side, and laughingly force her to walk around and around for hours. Katie wanted to leave. And like so many Europeans at the end of the nineteenth century, Liebe felt that immigration to America might provide a chance for happiness. Liebe found money to buy passage for her youngest child and, when Katie Friedman was twelve years old, she

Katie and Benjamin Reiter's wedding photograph, 1890. Photograph courtesy of Jonnie Stahl.

traveled alone to make her home in the United States.

The first time she tried to board a ship in Le Havre, she was turned away for being an unaccompanied child. Independent and inventive, she solved that problem: she waited until she saw a family with many children, attached herself to them, and quietly boarded. When Katie arrived at Ellis Island, she was met by Uncle Jacob who came down to "the boat" regularly, looking for friends and relatives. She went with him to Newark, New Jersey, where she worked in his grocery store. She was introduced to Benjamin Reiter, whom she married in 1890, when she was seventeen. The Reiters moved to McKeesport, Pennsylvania, a steel-mill town, just outside of Pittsburgh. Once settled in McKeesport, and pregnant, Katie re-turned her mother's favor. She sent money to Europe for passage. In 1891, Liebe, with her daughter Amelia and son Ephraim, joined the Reiters in Pennsylvania. Later that year, Katie's first-born, Adolph, died in early infancy. At about the same time, Ephraim drowned while boating on the Youghiogheny River, at the edge of McKees-port.

Katie and Benjamin Reiter with their seven children, c. 1907-1908. Theresa Reiter Gross is seated on her father's lap. Photograph courtesy of Jonnie Stahl.

Soon thereafter, less than a year from Katie's arrival in McKeesport, the two women started work on their quilt. Quilts made during periods of mourning are common. In the primary documents that survive, such as letters, journals, autobiographies and diaries, women refer to quilts made following the death of a loved one. A quiltmaker, in 1919, said:

> Mother had fourteen children, but only my brother and I lived. Some did not live long enough to be named; but there were two, twins, that lived a week, and she named them Rose and Roselle. I think she grieved for them more than for all the others. They were buried in coffins dug out of pine logs. . . .The field was plowed up the next year, and she lost track of their graves; they didn't have money for burying stones in those days, you know, and she wanted to keep them in mind somehow, so she made up the pattern of the twin roses. Her stitches are finer on this quilt than on any of the others, and she never let anyone use it or touch a hand to it.[2]

In the nineteenth century, when four out of ten children died before the age of six, quilts and quiltmaking played an important part in the rituals that surrounded death and dying. Quilts were made at bedsides during final illnesses. They were made as linings for caskets, and even served as burying cloths on overland journeys. Widows in mourning sometimes made quilts out of black and white fabrics. The process of quiltmaking helped women reconcile themselves to the loss of someone they dearly loved or depended upon. A quilt could take many hours to make and, during this time, a woman could remember, mourn, and eventually find comfort and resolution.

We can only speculate on what happened to Katie and Liebe through those mournful hours, what passed between them as they designed and sewed their special quilt. Did they share and grieve, sustained and consoled by the repetitive stitches of their quilting? How healing it must have been to have that time together. Somehow, out of their mutual sorrow, they created a quilt full of vibrant color. It is especially touching that this mourning quilt is covered with images

traditionally associated with growth (vines), life (tree of life), industry (hands) and hope and renewal (butterflies).

These mothers, whose European Jewish pasts did not include such needlework, created a quilt of love and life memorializing the lifeless boys and helping to heal their own grief. My own grandmothers brought crochet, knitting and embroidery with them from Poland and Russia when they came to America, around 1900, but no patchwork, no quilting. In a limited sampling, I found no other Jews whose European-born ancestors had made quilts. Since quiltmaking is generally regarded as an American form, most European-born women learned the skill here. Yet Jews tended to congregate in large cities, associating almost exclusively with other Jews. For most, quiltmaking was an invisible, alien craft. How did Katie come to make quilts, when so many other Jewish grandmothers did not? Could the difference be the result of her assimilation with her "American" neighbors?

I soon found family members who recalled that both Katie and her husband spoke English with almost no accent. My grandmothers, by contrast, still speak with very heavy accents, and one of them has never learned to read or write English. In McKeesport, a town with a relatively small Jewish

population, Benjamin was a highly successful insurance salesman; he and Katie were mixing with their American neighbors. Jonnie Stahl, another of Katie and Benjamin's grandchildren, told me that the Reiters were proud to have had the first automobile in McKeesport, evidence of their modern inclinations. "Katie was an orthodox Jew," Jonnie recalls, "but definitely an assimilated one."

It is likely, then, that Katie was exposed to quilts and quiltmaking by her neighbors in Newark, and had already begun to practice the art before her arrival in McKeesport. Indeed, this Reiter quilt shares some characteristics with the quilts of German-Americans, especially in its boldness, color, and some of its symbols. Newark, where Katie lived for six years before moving to McKeesport, and where she probably learned the basics of quiltmaking, was de-

scribed by Mary Lamb in an 1860 issue of *Harper's* as a "German town."[3] At the turn of the century, there were twenty breweries in Newark with names like Weidemeyer and Friedenham, two major daily newspapers printed in German, a German Presbyterian Church and a German hospital. It was "as German as Milwaukee, more German than Philadelphia."[4]

Most of the images which appear on the Reiter quilt are typical of Pennsylvania

German appliques — flowers, fruit, leaves and vines. Less commonly used are the animal forms Katie chose, such as cats, peacocks and hummingbirds. Although we must be cautious when imparting meaning to symbols used in quilts, it seems likely that the bucking bull and the calico dogs do more than resolve design problems; they are also pictures which one might associate with little boys. The most distinguishing images,

though, are the two proud horse-and-riders. Equestrians, either in military or civilian garb, appear quite regularly in the painted folk art of the Pennsylvania Dutch, but they are rarely seen in quilts. Reiter means "knight" or "rider" and refers to an Austrian ancestor of Benjamin who returned from war a hero, and after whom the family was named. The family believes that Katie made the riders, in black cloth, to represent and commemorate the two lost boys. Black is rarely used in applique quilts, and seems appropriate for these two figures. But what about the three other black pieces — a stylized rocking horse and two of the elephants? Was the choice random, made for aesthetic reasons, or did these figures have particular symbolic significance? As more family history is uncovered, we may someday find answers to these questions.

No one remembers how the quilt was

used until Leba's birth in 1933. It was then that Katie did something most unusual. She cut a strip out of her masterpiece and re-sewed the pieces into a crib quilt for the first-born of her youngest child, Theresa. Nobody knows why Katie did this, but Leba, let us not forget, was named for the other quiltmaker, Katie's mother. Leba remembers the crib quilt being laid on her bed as "a very special treat" when, at seven, she returned home after a tonsillectomy. Traditionally, quilts known as "sick quilts" were used to entertain, cheer and teach children about their families' histories. The quilt remained in three pieces for the next forty-three years. A maturing Leba, busy with life, forgot the quilt. In 1976, when she took a quilting class, she had what she thought was the novel idea of making a quilt with her mother. Leba called her and suggested they collaborate on a quilt. She was surprised when her mother said that they should "put the family quilt back together."

And so it has been. Leba began uncovering memories, contacting relatives, asking questions and making connections. It has been a very exciting process. More and more relatives are involved in digging up information, exploring issues raised in their search. As the pieces of the Reiter quilt have been rejoined, Leba has seen, for the first time, the entire album quilt, and the family is stitching together more and more of its own rich history.

Katie Reiter's quilt is a remarkable object, but its function and meaning go far beyond the visual and utilitarian. In its imaginative design, the quilt reminds us of the independent and resourceful twelve-year-old who left home alone to make her way in a new land. In quiltmaking she found a creative form characterized by tradition and continuity, concerns especially meaningful to an immigrant. Making the quilt with her mother after their mutual tragedies, she participated in two traditional aspects of the craft: interaction between female members of a family, and the process of anticipating, preparing for and, as in Katie's case, resolving major transitions and changes. The quilt reflects Katie's values as well. The image of the horseman is an homage to family tradition. The cutting of the quilt for her grandchild celebrates birth and pays tribute to her mother for whom the child was named. The quilt is a legacy. It is an archive of personal, familial and cultural information. Katie Reiter never wrote about herself but, in working her quilt, she has left us a diary of her life, written by needle.

⁂

JULIE SILBER is a lecturer and author on the subject of antique American quilts. She has been the co-curator of several major exhibitions, including one she organized for the Oakland (California) Museum in 1981, entitled "American Quilts: A Handmade Legacy." For ten years, she was co-owner with Linda Reuther of Mary Strickler's Quilt Gallery in San Rafael, California.

THE AUTHOR wishes to thank Theresa Reiter Gross, Jonnie Stahl and Leba Wine. This article would not have been possible without their generous help.

REFERENCE LIST

1. Arthur Schlesinger, introduction to *Pioneer Women*, by Joanna L. Stratton (New York: Simon & Schuster, 1981).

2. "Patchwork Romance," *House Beautiful*, 10 Jan. 1919, p. 24.

3. Charles Cummings, Chief Librarian, Newark Public Library Reference Division, Newark, N.J., telephone conversation with the author, 21 Sept. 1982.

4. *Ibid.*

Free Spirit in the West

By Michael Kile

To get to the Esprit Collection, you drive through San Francisco's warehouse district, past semi-trailer trucks unloading goods that have just come off the ships docked in the Bay. It is a typical warehouse district, perhaps a little cleaner than most. As you turn onto Minnesota Street and climb a slight hill, you see a low red brick warehouse. The building is architecturally like many of its neighbors, but that is where the similarities cease. Its front is lined by shade trees, and a large, colorful banner flies overhead. A single glass door tells you that you are at Esprit de Corp, one of America's fastest growing women's apparel designers and manufacturers, and the home of one of this country's major quilt collections. Here at Esprit's world headquarters, and in its showrooms worldwide, hangs a collection of over two hundred Amish quilts available for public viewing in rooms ranging from a dining area with a full-time chef to an employees' gymnasium.

On a weekday when the windsurfing on San Francisco Bay is bad or the rapids of a Northern California river are too low for kayaking, Doug Tompkins, who founded Esprit de Corp with his wife, Susie, can be found in jeans and plaid shirt, helping direct this multi-national company. Around him, and around all who work

THE COLLECTOR

here, are Amish quilts. Everywhere. In fact, it is difficult to find a spot in this three-story, open-spaced building where an Amish quilt isn't visible. Tompkins has been the impetus behind many of Esprit's innovations, not the least of which is the quilt collection.

The collection was begun in 1972, when Tompkins bought a non-Amish red-and-white baskets quilt. His second purchase was an Amish Sunshine and Shadow, and his third was a Lancaster County (Pennsylvania) Amish Diamond in the Square. These three quilts help tell the story of this unusual collection.

By 1975, Tompkins had collected over sixty-five quilts, and Esprit de Corp was being recognized for its personal, innovative clothing designs that sold in an affordable price range. As now, the quilts adorned the walls of the offices, workrooms, and even the shipping department. In January of that year, however, an overnight fire gutted the building, destroying nearly everything in it, including the Esprit quilt collection and the red-and-white baskets quilt.

There is a classic story of Tompkins arriving at the scene of the fire. It is said that his first question was, "Is everyone safe?" When told that, miraculously, there were no injuries, his second question was not about damage to designs or equipment but, "How about the quilts?" The answer to the second question was devastating.

Everything in the warehouse had been lost to the flames. "That was a terrible year," Tompkins remembers. "We weren't sure we would make it, but everyone pulled together. The staff was incredible."

Many people wondered what would happen to Esprit and to Doug and Susie Tompkins. They didn't have to wait very long for an answer. Within eleven months, Esprit was back in its refurbished building and Tompkins had bought himself a quilt to start rebuilding his collection. Walking into 900 Minnesota Street today, one would never guess this young, thriving business and its imposing quilt collection have already lived two lives.

Since 1975, Tompkins has collected every quilt displayed at Esprit except those which had fortunately survived the fire by being off-premises. This in itself is a feat to be admired. At a time when this country, particularly the East Coast, was gobbling up Amish quilts as fast as they appeared on the market, Tompkins was methodically and aggressively grouping his collection. "There's a lot of competition out there for quilts. You have to be persistent," Tompkins admits. "Persistent" might be an understatement in Tompkins' case. The collection has grown far beyond most collectors' dreams. It contains works from every Amish settlement, and is at a point where the weeding-out process is a task in and of itself. For example, Tompkins recently decided to deaccession all

non-Amish quilts. Like most serious collectors, Tompkins has gone through three stages: discovery and an exuberance for quilts in general; acquisition and the sometimes insatiable desire to possess; and discrimination with its painful process of reassessment. The second quilt he purchased, the Amish Sunshine and Shadow, has been sold, a victim of reappraisal. His third purchase, the Amish Diamond in the Square, has found a permanent place in the collection and hangs in the gymnasium at the San Francisco headquarters.

Those visiting this landmark collection are immediately struck by the predominance of strong color and graphic power. There are few subtleties in this collection. It is bold and brassy, reflecting the collector's obsession with innovative design and interesting color treatments. A majority of the quilts are outstandingly rare examples possessing these qualities. "Ninety-five per cent of this collection is graphics and color," adds Tompkins. "The other five per cent is history, quilting and techniques. Give me a choice between a great graphic quilt with no history and a mediocre one with a complete family history, and I'll take the great graphic piece every time." Any criticism of the collection has been based upon this predilection. Some quilt historians, dealers and collectors have found fault with Tompkins' disinterest in the historical and cultural context of these Amish works. One critic said, "The quilts have

conservation-minded way in which it is mounted (Velcro, sewn to all four sides of each quilt, is used in all installations) are awe-inspiring, and visitors' reactions are extremely positive. There are, after all, few places in this country where a large quilt collection, adequately displayed, can be viewed on any weekday. In sheer numbers alone, this quilt collection ranks among the greatest ever assembled.

There seems to be little disagreement over one of the collection's strongest points: its owner's willingness to share his treasures with an appreciative world. Seldom does a day go by without a few individuals or groups touring the Esprit offices and the collection. "I feel we should share this collection with truly interested people. And we try to accommodate all visitors. Naturally, we work here, and that has to come first. I can't have the staff's pri-

been ripped from their culture and displayed as cold designs in a corporate setting. They are no longer documents of people's lives."

But such criticism does not deter Tompkins. "I collect quilts because I like them. And what I like is their strong visual appeal. I'm not really very interested in how many spools of thread it took to make a particular quilt; I'm interested in the end result. Does it appeal to me? If it does, I buy it."

Although some quilt enthusiasts may disagree with the collection's focus, its impact is nearly universal. The collection and the

vacy and creative energy sapped by intruders. Most visitors, however, are very thoughtful viewers. They don't enter occupied offices and disrupt meetings. They work around us and we work around them." The Esprit Collection reflects a strength shared by most corporate quilt collections. Although such collections have their detractors, no one can dispute the advantage they share with Esprit: more people are seeing these quilts — and enjoying them — than would ever see them in private or museum collections.

Tompkins views his collection as a major event in his life. It is a

reflection of his strong personal taste. Like all accomplished or developing collectors, he has made certain that his collection reflects *his* personal choice, not that of advisers, dealers or critics. As he proceeds, his passion does not subside, but is balanced by a desire for excellence. "My major emphasis at this point is on upgrading the collection," Tompkins admits. "I've seen more quilts than most people see in a lifetime. Through collecting I discovered that I like Amish quilts best because, as a group, they are most successful in uniting strong color and design. As a result, I'm getting rid of all my non-Amish quilts. And some of them," he adds, "are beauties. I just had to decide what kind of collection I wanted. When I'd decided that, the other decisions fell into place. I'm going to be collecting for many years to come, but at this point I'm only after the unusual. I've owned my share of Diamonds." And he adds, smiling, "Now I only want the great ones."

If the Esprit Collection is any indication, he'll get them.

The Esprit Collection's home is 900 Minnesota Street, San Francisco 94107, telephone 415/648-6900. Individual tours of the collection are self-administered and free of charge. Group tours are conducted by a member of the Esprit staff, and a fee is charged. Appointments should be made for all tours.

COLLECTING QUILT DATA:

HISTORY FROM STATISTICS

QUILTS have finally claimed a distinct place in the roster of what is called American folk art. However, because of their hybrid nature, they are part of a discrete genre. A blend of art and function, they belong to that group of objects whose basic intent was utilitarian and whose art is in their form and ornamental decoration. Other examples of such objects are tavern signs, painted furniture, decorated pottery and embroidered textiles.

The great resurgence of interest in quilts during the last decade grew from the recognition of quilts as designed, or art, objects, and focused initially on pieced quilts. These had been largely neglected, except as supposed examples of ingenious thrift. In museums, restorations, exhibitions and books on American art, the emphasis was more on workmanship, on "best quilts" (usually applique), and on quilts with great age or historical importance. Interest in quilt design was created by changing their function, by moving them from beds to the walls of museums and galleries, where they became non-functional art objects. This shift enabled people interested in art but not necessarily in American art, folk or otherwise, to assess quilts as color, form and line. The benefits have been a reawakening of interest in all American quilts and the initiation of the modern era of quilt design, in which the form has been carried in new directions by gifted amateurs and professionals.

As soon as quilts were acknowledged as art — were legitimized for many — they became the subject of intense study. A good number of books, articles, exhibitions, lectures, films and seminars have been devoted to them. Some are designed for those interested mainly in the craft or the socio-economic importance, others for those interested primarily in the art. More and more efforts are being made to study the subject in a systematic and serious manner. The project undertaken this past year in Kentucky, "Time Capsules: The Kentucky Quilt Project 1800-1900," is an example. A well-organized attempt was made to draw out quilts from the entire state for study. Fourteen Quilt Days, well-advertised in advance by local newspapers and quilting groups, were held in major cities around the state. Recruited volunteers helped with the crowds and the days' activities. Quilts were photographed and their vital statistics and family histories were recorded. Organizers discussed each quilt with its owner, urging proper preservation. The exercise was very successful. Some eleven hundred quilts were studied and their features noted; an exhibition and book documenting forty-four of the quilts followed. (See this issue's *Showcase* for an example.)

Serious attention has recently been given to particular types of quilts (the exhibition, "Baltimore Album Quilts," at the Baltimore, New York Metropolitan and Houston Museums, and the exhibition of nineteenth-century crib and doll quilts, "Small Endearments," at the Los Angeles Municipal Art

Gallery, for example). "American Quilts: A Handmade Legacy" at the Oakland (California) Museum investigated quilts as a part of personal history, their role in women's lives in the past and, in the person of seven contemporary quiltmakers, the present. Many more studies, by region and type, of individual makers' work, of technique, of quilts in their historical setting, are needed and will follow.

Edge: an example of home-cut binding in a straight cut. (Detail from a pieced cotton Pennsylvania wall pocket, c. 1870.)

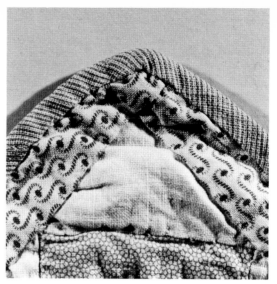

Edge: an example of home-cut binding in a bias cut. (Detail from a pieced cotton Pennsylvania crib quilt, c. 1870.)

As such studies are conducted, as quilts are sought out, looked at and handled, a priceless chance to collect data of technical, aesthetic and historical interest is created. *Any* quilt can give up valuable hard data on construction techniques, materials, design and dimensions; and if the quilts are known in their geographical and/or historical context, the value of the hard data is greatly increased, links are made with other data, and important specific history is added.

It would be difficult to overestimate the value of such data. Quilts are the most significant American artifacts still owned in any number by the families of their makers. While quilting is often thought of as an anonymous art, it is actually considerably less so than are most American craft forms. In fact, it is probably the least anonymous; there are many, many more known quiltmakers than craftsmen of furniture, glass,

pottery, folk painting or sculpture. Quilts from the first half of the nineteenth century are rare; yet even from that period the makers of many and their histories are known, and the number of later quilts with ascertainable histories increases dramatically. A quick glance at any other field of American craft or folk art will indicate how few artists we actually can identify. The historical reason for this is that until recently, with the rise of the cult of the creative personality, there was very little tradition for recording the authorship of craft products. (Even professional or semi-professional artists of the eighteenth and nineteenth centuries often did not sign their

work.) Quilts are different. First, a fair number are signed, and many dated. Second, as was found in the Kentucky project, many quilts are in the hands of descendants who know a good bit about the makers' histories. In addition, many quilts have gone to public and private collections with their creators' identity and family history intact. It seems obvious that the affection in which quilts were held, their importance to their makers and those to whom they were passed, has helped preserve histories and identities.

The value of such information to America's social history needs no emphasis. What, though, of the other sides, the technical and aesthetic? Details of construction and technique are of interest on a number of levels. First, it is often in the fine details of edging, assembly, sewing, choice of materials and quilting—the craft—that the maker reveals her temperament, her circumstances, and her time and place. In addition, art and structure are as inextricably interrelated in a quilt as they are in any object with a planned aesthetic. Just as in painting, great craft does not ensure great art, nor does a disregard of craft and conventional imagery guarantee a vital result, a successful "primitive" work.

The craft is of equal interest to the general study of quilts. For example, of the forty-four quilts selected for exhibition in the Kentucky project, seven were appliques. Of these, four have a special edge, I think the most elegant ever used on American quilts: a green edging binds, at its inner edge, a cording covered in red cloth. I have seen this sort of edging in other areas, but a good percentage of Kentucky "best" applique quilts seem to have it. Is this a regional characteristic? Is its incidence in applique quilts the same in other geographical areas? Where did it begin? Why always red within green? Is that color scheme the same in other areas? If so, does this indicate a common source for the trait, or a conservative bent among makers of such quilts? Another example might be quilt backs. In a given period, what percentage of quilts had whole-cloth backs of white cotton? What percentage had printed cottons? Was the back whole or pieced? If backs were pieced from bolt lengths, what width were the sections? How much handspun, as compared to manufactured cloth, was used for backs?

Such information would help scholars produce increasingly complex and accurate studies of quilts. It would help us focus on particular concerns, regions, types and materials. Larger trends would slowly become visible. Scholars are becoming more interested in the socio-economic significance of quilts. A gathering of such statistics would help them investigate, for instance, how work and time factors influenced quilt-making and design; how much piecing was done by machines after they were well-established; and how many quilts with machine-run edges were pieced by hand. Secondarily, this sort of information is significant to other areas of study, such as rural economics, textile use, the development of the textile industry and fashion.

To be of most value in the study of quilts and in other fields of inquiry, the information must be collected, stored and indexed in a manner which makes it easily accessible: the greatest possible flexibility in calling up and cross-indexing it is the goal. Of course, computers are part of the answer; it no longer makes sense to collect detailed information on any subject and not organize it in such a way that it can be committed, now or later, to a computer system. Computers will be used more and more in the analysis of art. Museums are utilizing computer systems to record detailed information on their holdings. The computer is being used increasingly by scholars to sort such information. This past year the Yale University Art Gallery mounted "The Work of Many Hands," an exhibition and detailed examination of American card tables, concentrating on regional characteristics. The analyses were based on computer studies of four hundred tables organized by an industrial psychologist on Yale's faculty, Benjamin A. Hewitt, who is interested in

Edge: an example where the back material is turned over the top. (Detail from a pieced cotton Pennsylvania quilt, c. 1880.)

American furniture. Using his expertise in pattern recognition gained from his psychological studies, and an additional background in cryptography, he coded 176 pieces of key information about card tables. The study enabled Hewitt and his associates to make discoveries about regional characteristics of tables, the specialized manufacture and distribution of inlays and the regional use of specific woods. Information was both quantitative and qualitative. There is no question that more such studies will be done, yielding equally fruitful results. Masses of data which one knew might contain extremely valuable information, but which without computers might be too forbidding to attack, will be systematically collected and sifted. A new generation of scholars who have grown up using computers — and those in the older generation willing to learn how — will undertake such quantitative studies as a matter of course. They will be aided by the increasing availability, sophistication and economy of the hardware.

A great interest of mine for some years has been the possibility of compiling an organized and growing body of factual information about American quilts and, at the same time, finding a way to gather and manage such information as it is generated by field studies. The questions were how to collect such data, how to store it and how to retrieve it. To be widely useful or even workable, the information-gathering has to be intelligible to people with no quilt expertise. I thought a standard questionnaire could be compiled, one which would enable anyone with some common sense and the ability to look at an object to examine a quilt and list its most important characteristics. It also seemed clear to me that the questionnaire could be designed so that the information gathered could be committed to a computer system. Such a questionnaire could be used for both institutional and private collections, and could be an adjunct to any quilt studies. If someone were, for instance, working toward an exhibition of applique quilts and were willing to fill in a fact sheet on all the quilts examined, he would create documents of use beyond the confines of his project.

Naturally, there are problems. Some are technical and require the advice of computer specialists: how the information should be collected; what hardware/software combination will accomplish one's goals; and how to ensure compatibility with other systems. Other problems revolve around the questionnaire. Quilts would be examined by people of varying expertise. Thus, information which required educated judgments, such as age, would be of much less value

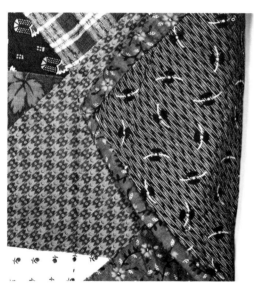

Edge: an example where the top material is turned over the back. (Detail from a pieced cotton Pennsylvania quilt, c. 1875.)

Edge: an example of home-loomed tape binding. (Detail from a pieced cotton New York quilt, c. 1840.)

than hard data. On the other hand, the bulk of the data of interest, such as size, how the edge is finished, if the quilt is signed or dated and the recording of documentation or family history require no particular knowledge.

Edge: an example of a typical Pennsylvania Amish home-cut wool binding. (Detail from a Lancaster County quilt, c. 1900.)

Accompanying instruction sheets would give guidance for making judgments, and there would certainly be photographic aids. Close-up pictures of stitching by hand and machine, for instance, should help the examiner determine which was used. Different block types would be illustrated. Each category in which complex judgments had to be made, such as age, would have "can't tell" as a possible response, to discourage guesswork. Pattern is also of great importance but presents difficult problems. It would be practically impossible to design questions whose answers would give an accurate picture of even the less complex quilt designs. Traditional pattern names are not usable, because the same design is labeled differently in different places. I have listed in the questionnaire a number of overall formats (Album quilts and Framed Center quilts, for example) and will include photographs of typical examples so that such types are quickly identified. These special types comprise, however, but a small percentage of quilts, and even type identification gives us little visual information about a given quilt. A photograph of each quilt, plus close-ups of a block or other significant details (a name, date or particularly fine quilting, for example), is of course the optimum solution. Thus, instructions for taking pictures would be included with the questionnaire. Or a small visual reference of standard types might be compiled and the examiner would indicate the design closest

to the quilt under study. In many cases, however, no information about design would be derived, but other information would still be of great interest. And where the investigator had the expertise and facilities to answer all questions accurately, extremely valuable documents would be created.

What follows is a possible questionnaire. Samples of the sort of photographic aids we will use have been included in this article. A good many adjustments will no doubt be necessary. Grading Systems, Inc., which designed a data storage system for me, will monitor the developing program so flaws are not built in at the start. Field testing will then no doubt reveal errors and possibilities not envisioned. To a future issue of *The Quilt Digest* I hope to submit a tested questionnaire in its entirety, a discussion of how the data might be stored and made available to scholars and perhaps a few results gleaned from the first trials. I hope this working questionnaire will create a dialogue from which will come improvements in its form and usefulness.

JONATHAN HOLSTEIN is a quilt historian and pioneer in the rediscovery of American quilts. He has lectured and written widely on the subject. From the collection formed by him and his wife, Gail van der Hoof, the 1971 Whitney Museum exhibition "Abstract Design in American Quilts" was drawn. Many other exhibitions, both here and abroad, followed. His book, *The Pieced Quilt*, is a standard text in the field.

QUILT DATA QUESTIONNAIRE

A FEW NOTES
ON COMPOSING
THE QUESTIONNAIRE

The questionnaire derives from a structural analysis of American quilts. While there is seemingly a great variety of quilt types, their actual differences are few; the basic structure of a quilt (top, filler and back, tied or stitched together) remains constant. Distinctions among quilts are found largely in the top. Two types, tops of whole-cloth foundation (with or without additions) and assembled tops, account for all quilts. The importance of differences among tops is apparent: they make one quilt look different from another. All other differences are in details of construction and decoration, such as assembly, edging, sewing, choice of materials and quilting. These are, of course, no less important; they give the quilt its character and feel.

After a number of trials, I determined that declarative statements are simplest and most understandable. These can be responded to (some with multiple choices) if they apply, or ignored if they do not. I have used this form wherever possible.

QUESTIONNAIRE

Date_____

Examiner's Name_____

Address_____

City_____

State_____Zip_____

Telephone (_____) _____

Registry No._____

Date Entered_____

By Whom_____

_____

Owner's Name_____

Address_____

City_____

State_____Zip_____

Telephone (_____) _____

Owner's No._____

Accession

Information_____

_____

QUILT

Date made_____Estimation_____Can't tell [ ]

Place made_____Place collected_____

Maker's name_____

Overall size _____ x _____ inches _____ x _____ cm

Condition: Like new [ ]   Almost new [ ]   Moderate use [ ]

Much use [ ]   Worn [ ]

Exhibited:_____

Reproduced:_____

I. Top
  1. Structure and type
    a. The top is made in one piece [ ] and is in white [ ] solid colors [ ] patterned cloth [ ]. It has applique [ ] reverse applique [ ] crewel [ ] cross stitch [ ] other embroidery [ ] (specify:_____) or stencil [ ] work. The top is made in several pieces of the same material, but looks like one piece [ ]. How many pieces?_____ What are their widths?_____
    OR
    b. The top is assembled in:
    [ ] Block style   or [ ] Mosaic style
      [ ] Pieced   [ ] Baby block
      [ ] Applique   [ ] Hexagonal
                                       [ ] Star
                                       [ ] Other

    or [ ] Random style   or [ ] Openwork
       [ ] Crazy   [ ] Yo-Yo
         [ ] Silk   [ ] Cathedral
         [ ] Velvet
       [ ] Cotton
       [ ] Wool

  2. Design
    a. The top's pattern is_____. Can't tell [ ]
       Photo attached [ ] Sketch attached [ ]
    b. Type of whole-cloth tops (check one, if applicable):
    [ ] Hawaiian   [ ] Linsey-woolsey
    [ ] Revenue   [ ] Historical/
    [ ] Presentation   Commemorative/
    [ ] Landscape/Narrative   Political
    [ ] Calligraphic   [ ] Using specially printed
    [ ] Photo   materials
    [ ] Button
    OR
    c. Type of assembled tops (check one, if applicable):
    [ ] Log Cabin type block   [ ] Pennsylvania Amish
      [ ] Standard Log Cabin   [ ] Center Diamond
      [ ] Courthouse Steps   [ ] Bars
      [ ] Pineapple   [ ] Sunshine and Shadow
                                   [ ] Bordered center
                                   [ ] Other (specify :_____
                                       _____)

[ ] Autograph quilts   [ ] Premium Patch   [ ] Historical/
  [ ] Friendship   [ ] Strip   Commemorative/
  [ ] Friendship Album   [ ] Framed Center   Political
  [ ] Album   [ ] Postage Stamp   [ ] Uses
  [ ] Baltimore Album   [ ] Landscape/Narrative   specially
  [ ] Revenue   [ ] Photo   printed
                                                      materials
[ ] Cigar band
    d. Borders
       How many borders are there?_____Their widths (from the quilt's outer edge in) are_____.
       The quilt is specially shaped with a four-poster flap [ ] with rounded corners at one end [ ].
    e. Set (if this is a block style quilt)
       The blocks are set square [ ] set as diamonds [ ].
       They are joined together [ ] separated by sashes [ ].
    f. Sashes
       The sashes are made of uncut strips [ ] pieced strips [ ].
       If pieced in strips, they are in the same material [ ] different materials [ ]. The material(s) is/are in solid color(s) [ ] patterned [ ].
    g. Sewing
       The top is sewn by hand [ ] machine [ ] both [ ]. If both, specify where each type of stitching is used:_____.
       _____
    h. Written information
       The top is signed [ ] in the quilting [ ] in ink [ ] stamped in ink [ ] in embroidery [ ]. Signature:_____ in ink [ ] in stencil [ ]. The top is initialed [ ] in the quilting _____. The top is initialed [ ] in the quilting [ ] in ink [ ] stamped in ink [ ] in stencil [ ] in embroidery [ ]. The initials are_____. The top is dated [ ] in the quilting [ ] in ink [ ] stamped in ink [ ] in stencil [ ] in embroidery [ ]. The date is_____. The top contains the name of a place [ ] in the quilting [ ] in ink [ ] stamped in ink [ ] in stencil [ ] in embroidery [ ]. The place is_____.
    i. Additional decoration is done in embroidery [ ] drawing in ink [ ] 3-D appliques [ ] painting [ ] other [ ]. If other, specify:_____.

j. Materials
   The materials are cotton [ ] (glazed [ ] chintz [ ]) wool
   [ ] linen [ ] silk [ ] velvet [ ] synthetic [ ]. If
   synthetic, the type is _____. Can't tell the
   material [ ]. The material is handmade [ ] commercial [ ]
   can't tell [ ].

II. Edge
1. Way edge is finished
   a. Binding
      [ ] Home-cut   or [ ] Tape   or [ ] Ribbon
         [ ] Straight-cut   [ ] Home-loomed
         [ ] Bias-cut   [ ] Commercial
         [ ] Cording   [ ] Can't tell
      The binding is made of cotton [ ] wool [ ] linen [ ] silk
      [ ] velvet [ ] synthetic [ ] can't tell [ ].
      If there is no separate binding material, the edges are
      tucked in [ ] the back material is turned over the top [ ]
      the top material is turned over the back [ ].
      The edge is shaped in a straight line [ ] sawtooth [ ]
      scallop [ ] other [ ]. If other, specify:_____.
      The width of the binding is_____.
   b. Fringe
      There is a fringe which is woven [ ] netting [ ] crocheted
      [ ]. It is handmade [ ] commercial [ ] can't tell [ ].
      The width of the fringe is_____.
   c. Ruffle
      There is a ruffle which is whole cloth [ ] pieced [ ]. It
      had added decoration in embroidery [ ] in applique [ ]
      other [ ] (specify:_____).
      It is made of cotton [ ] wool [ ] linen [ ] silk [ ] velvet
      [ ] synthetic [ ] can't tell [ ].
      It is sewn by hand [ ] machine [ ] both [ ]. If both,
      specify where each type of stitching is used:_____
      _____. The width of the ruffle is_____.

III. Back
1. Construction
   [ ] One piece or [ ] Pieced in the or [ ] Pieced in different
              same material   materials
         [ ] In strips   [ ] In strips
           How many?   [ ] In a pattern
         _____ Their widths [ ] Other (describe):

   The back is pieced and sewn by hand [ ] machine [ ]. Its
   material is cotton [ ] glazed cotton [ ] wool [ ] linen [ ]
   silk [ ] velvet [ ] synthetic [ ] other [ ] (specify:_____
   _____) can't tell [ ]. This material was made by hand
   [ ] machine [ ] can't tell [ ]. The material(s) is/are all
   white [ ] solid color(s) [ ] patterned [ ]. If solid
   color(s), specify:_____.

IV. Quilting
   The quilt is tufted or tied [ ] has quilting sewn by hand [ ] has
   quilting sewn by machine [ ]. The number of stitches per inch
   are _____. Describe quilting designs (from the outer edge to
   the center):_____
   There is contour quilting [ ].
   There is raised work [ ]. It is stuffed[ ] padded [ ] cording [ ]
   pressed [ ] raised but can't tell which type [ ]. Give details
   regarding designs and areas affected:_____

V. Filling
   The filling is made of cotton [ ] wool [ ] synthetic [ ] blanket
   [ ] another quilt [ ] can't tell [ ] there is no filling [ ].
   If the filling is made of cotton, it has some seeds [ ] a few
   seeds [ ]. The thickness of the quilt at its thinnest point is
   _____. The thickness of the quilt at its thickest point is_____.

Other Books from

THE
QUILT DIGEST
PRESS

AVAILABLE IN SEPTEMBER 1986

*T*HE ART QUILT by Penny McMorris and Michael Kile. The creator/producer of the extremely popular PBS television series "Quilting" and "Quilting II" and author of *Crazy Quilts* joins the editor of *The Quilt Digest* to present the first fully comprehensive book about the contemporary art quilt.

Their thorough examination of the events which led to the emergence of the art quilt extends back to the arts and crafts movement of the late nineteenth century. They recount events during the 1920's and 1930's quilt revival and discuss how the turbulent 1960's influenced the current crafts revival. Their focus encompasses modern art, how it has affected today's quilt artists and how quilts, in turn, have influenced artists working in other media.

Based upon their interpretation of these various influences, McMorris and Kile chronicle the emergence of the contemporary art quilt and its creators, discussing the current state of the art, showing where quilt artists have been and where they might lead in the future.

The authors are joined by the world's leading quilt artists—Pauline Burbidge, Nancy Crow, Deborah Felix, Gayle Fraas and Duncan Slade, Jean Hewes, Michael James, Ruth McDowell, Terrie Hancock Mangat, Therese May, Jan Myers, Yvonne Porcella, Joan Schulze and Pam Studstill—who have spent the last two years creating quilts especially for this milestone book.

These never-before-seen quilts are the centerpiece of this extremely important fine art volume. Lavishly illustrated in full color and sumptuously designed, it is published in both paperback and hard-cover editions.

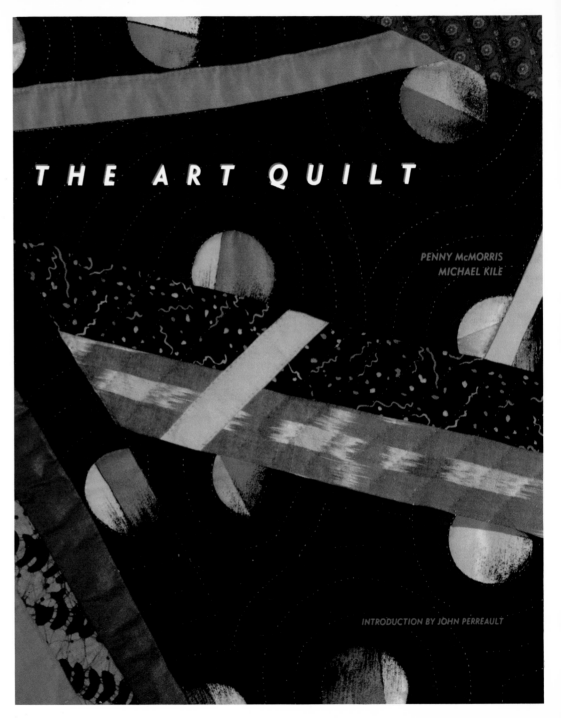

THE ART QUILT

PENNY McMORRIS
MICHAEL KILE

INTRODUCTION BY JOHN PERREAULT

THE QUILT DIGEST 2. Eighty pages with 60 color photographs and 17 black-and-white photographs and illustrations. Many rare quilts, plus a superb private collection, vintage photos of *Crazy* quilts in a Victorian home, a pioneer wife and her quilt, quilt care and conservation, Hawaiian Flag quilts. $12.95.

THE QUILT DIGEST 3. Eighty-eight pages with 93 color photographs. Dozens of exceptional quilts, plus Quaker quilts, formal Southern quilts from the Charleston (South Carolina) Museum collection, a short story about a wife and husband and their quilt, eccentric quilts, an Alabama pioneer and her quilts. $15.95.

THE QUILT DIGEST 4. Eighty-eight pages with 75 color and 8 black-and-white photographs. Articles include "Pine Tree Quilts" by Suellen Meyer; " 'Helping the Peoples to Help Themselves,' " the story of the Freedom Quilting Bee of Alabama, a black, self-help co-operative of quilters, by Nancy Callahan; "Quilts in Art" by Penny McMorris, in which the influence of quilts on contemporary art is aptly illustrated; "The Collector: On the Road," a look at the never-before-published quilts of a quilt dealer, by Michael Kile; "Old Maid, New Woman," accompanied by the "Old Maid" quilt her friends made for her, the true story of a nineteenth-century single woman who dedicated her life to the service of others, by Shelly Zegart; and "Showcase," Roderick Kiracofe's annual selection of beautiful antique and contemporary quilts. The fourth volume in our acclaimed series. $16.95.

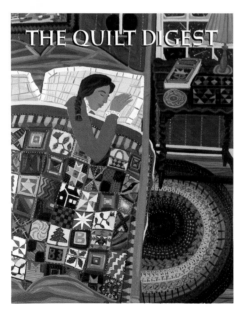

REMEMBER ME: Women & Their Friendship Quilts by Linda Otto Lipsett. One hundred and thirty-six pages with 112 color and 23 black-and-white photographs. A thorough examination of friendship quilts and an intimate portrait of seven nineteenth-century quiltmakers who made them, rendered in astonishing detail. A unique book that will transport you back into an earlier time. $19.95 paperback. $29.95 hard cover.

HOMAGE TO AMANDA by Edwin Binney, 3rd and Gail Binney-Winslow. Ninety-six pages with 71 color photographs. A great quilt collection bountifully illustrates this concise guide to the first two hundred years of American quiltmaking. Published by Roderick Kiracofe/R K Press and distributed exclusively by The Quilt Digest Press. $16.95.

Our Mailing List

If your name is not on our mailing list and you would like it to be, please write to us. We will be happy to add your name so that you will receive advance information about our forthcoming books.

Ordering Information

Thousands of quilt, antique, book and museum shops around the world carry the books we publish. Check with shops in your area. Or you may order books directly from us.

To order, send us your name, address, city, state and zip code. Tell us which books you wish to order and in what quantity. California residents add 6% sales tax. Finally, to the price of the books you order, add $1.75 for the first book and $1.00 for each additional book to cover postage and handling charges. Enclose your check made payable to *The Quilt Digest Press* and mail it, along with the above information, to Dept. D, 955 Fourteenth Street, San Francisco 94114.

Readers outside North America may have their orders shipped via air mail by including $8.00 for each book ordered. All orders must be accompanied by payment in U.S. dollars drawn on a U.S. bank.

Depending upon the season of the year, allow 4–6 weeks for delivery. Readers outside North America should allow several additional weeks for sea delivery.

We are happy to send gift books directly to recipients.

Wholesale information is available upon request.